IN THE

KINGDOM

OF THE

SEA

MONKEYS

An Imprint of HarperCollins*Publishers*

IN THE

KINGDOM

OF THE

SEA

MONKEYS

CAMPBELL MCGRATH

IN THE KINGDOM OF THE SEA MONKEYS. Copyright © 2012 by Campbell McGrath. All rights reserved. Printed in the United States of America. No part of this book may be used or reproduced in any manner whatsoever without written permission except in the case of brief quotations embodied in critical articles and reviews. For information address HarperCollins Publishers, 10 East 53rd Street, New York, NY 10022.

HarperCollins books may be purchased for educational, business, or sales promotional use. For information please write: Special Markets Department, HarperCollins Publishers, 10 East 53rd Street, New York, NY 10022.

FIRST EDITION

Designed by Suet Yee Chong

Library of Congress Cataloging-in-Publication Data has been applied for.

ISBN 978-0-06-211090-9

12 13 14 15 16   OV/RRD   10 9 8 7 6 5 4 3 2 1

for my teachers

ACKNOWLEDGMENTS

My thanks to the editors of the publications in which these poems first appeared:

American Poet, American Poetry Review, The Atlantic, Bat City Review, Burnside Review, Cent Journal, Connotation Press: An Online Artifact, The Fiddleback, Gulf Coast, Hinchas de Poesía, Huffington Post, Indiana Review, Kenyon Review, Knockout, New Ohio Review, The New Yorker, Northwest Review, Ocho, Ploughshares, Poetry, Poetry Northwest, Salmagundi, Slate, Smartish Pace, Southern Review, Sugarhouse Review, TriQuarterly, Tuesday: An Art Project, Virginia Quarterly Review.

"The Cattle Raid" was originally published in *Planet on the Table: Poets on the Reading Life,* Sarabande Books, edited by Sharon Bryan and William Olsen.

Several of these poems appeared in the chapbook *The Custodian & Other Poems,* published by floatingwolfquarterly.com.

"Books" is for Daniel Halpern.
"Notes on the Poem" is for Kevin Young.
"Minneapolis" is for Paul Westerberg.
"The Fly" is for C. K. Williams.
"The Mountain" is for Italo Calvino.
"Snake River, End of March" is for Robert Wrigley.

"The Custodian" is for John Lane.

"Poetry and the World" is for Denise Duhamel.

"Po Biz" is for Mark Halliday.

"The Burning Ship" is for Reg Gibbons.

"The Cattle Raid" is for Seamus Heaney.

CONTENTS

II

I

BOOKS

Books live in the mind like honey inside a beehive,
that ambrosial archive, each volume sealed in craft-made paper,
nutritive cells, stamen-fragrant, snug as apothecary jars.

Like fossilized trilobites, or skulls in a torch-lit catacomb
beneath an ancient city, Byzantium or Ecbatana,
or Paris at the end of April when vendors set their folding tables
filled with lily-of-the-valley beside every Métro entrance,

and the women, coming home from work or market,
scented already with the fugitive perfume of *muguets,*
carry hand-held bouquets like pale tapers
through the radiant, rain-washed streets at sunset.

And then it is night, half the world ruled by dreams
from which arise narrative forms—riddles, fables, myths—
as mist lifts from mountain valleys in autumn,
as steam belches from fumaroles in benthic trenches

to whose sulfuric cones strange life-forms cling,
chrome-green crabs and eyeless shrimp, soft-legged starfish
sung to sleep by that curious cousin of the hippopotamus,

the whale, who, having first evolved from ocean to land
in the ever-eventful Cretaceous, thought better of it,
returning, after millions of years, to scholarly contemplation
in the mesomorphic, metaphysical library of the sea.

EMILY AND WALT

I suppose we did not want for love.
They were considerate parents, if a bit aloof,

or more than a bit. He was a colossus
of enthusiasms, none of them us,

while she kissed our heads and mended socks
with a wistful, faraway look.

She might have been a little, well, daft.
And he—*Allons, my little ones,* he'd laugh,

then leave without us.
And those "friends" of his!

Anyway, he's gone off to "discover
himself" in San Francisco, or wherever,

while she's retired to the condo in Boca.
We worry, but she says she likes it in Florida;

she seems, almost, happy. I suppose they were
less care-givers than enablers,

they taught by example, reading for hours
in the draughty house and now the house is ours,

with its drawers full of junk and odd
lines of verse and stairs that ascend to God

knows where, belfries and gymnasia,
the chapel, the workshop, aviaries, atria—

we could never hope to fill it all.
Our voices are too small

for its silences, too thin to spawn an echo.
Sometimes, even now, when the night-wind blows

into the chimney flue
I start from my bed, calling out—"Hello,

Mom and Dad, is that you?"

SHOPPING FOR POMEGRANATES AT WAL-MART ON NEW YEAR'S DAY

Beneath a ten-foot-tall apparition of Frosty the Snowman
with his corncob pipe and jovial, over-eager, button-black eyes,
holding, in my palm, the leathery, wine-colored purse
of a pomegranate, I realize, yet again, that America is a country
about which I understand everything and nothing at all,
that this is life, this ungovernable air
in which the trees rearrange their branches, season after season,
never certain which configuration will bear the optimal yield
of sunlight and water, the enabling balm of nutrients,
that so too do Wal-Mart's ferocious sales managers
relentlessly analyze their end-cap placement, product mix
and shopper demographics, that this is the culture
in all its earnestness and absurdity, that it never rests,
that each day is an eternity and every night is New Year's Eve,
a cavalcade of B-list has-beens entirely unknown to me,
needy comedians and country singers in handsome Stetsons,
sitcom stars of every social trope and ethnic denomination,
pugilists and oligarchs, femmes fatales and anointed virgins
throat-slit in offering to the cannibal throng of Times Square.
Who are these people? I grow old. I lie unsleeping
as confetti falls, ash-girdled, robed in sweat and melancholy,
click-shifting from QVC to reality TV, strings of commercials
for breath freshener, debt reconsolidation, a new car
lacking any whisper of style or grace, like a final fetid gasp
from the lips of a dying Henry Ford, potato-faced actors
impersonating real people with real opinions

offered forth with idiot grins in the yellow, herniated studio light,

actual human beings, actual souls bought too cheaply.

That it never ends, O Lord, that it never ends!

That it is relentless, remorseless, and it is on right now.

That one sees it and sees it but sometimes it sees you, too,

cowering in a corner, transfixed by the crawler for the storm alert,

home videos of faces left dazed by the twister, the car bomb,

the war always beginning or already begun, always

the special report, the inside scoop, the hidden camera

revealing the mechanical lives of the sad, inarticulate people

we have come to know as "celebrities."

Who assigns such value, who chose these craven avatars

if not the miraculous hand of the marketplace

whose torn cuticles and gaudily painted fingernails resemble nothing

so much as our own? Where does the oracle reveal our truths

more vividly than upon that pixillated spirit-glass

unless it is here, in this tabernacle of homely merchandise,

a Copernican model of a money-driven universe

revolving around its golden omphalos, each of us summed

and subtotaled, integers in an equation of need and consumption,

desire and consummation, because Hollywood had it right all along,

the years are a montage of calendar pages and autumn leaves,

sheet music for a nostalgic symphony of which our lives comprise

but single trumpet blasts, single notes in the hullabaloo,

or even less—we are but motes of dust in that atmosphere

shaken by the vibrations of time's imperious crescendo.

That it never ends, O Lord. That it goes on,

without pause or cessation, without pity or remorse.

That we have willed it into existence, dreamed it into being.

That it is our divine monster, our factotum, our scourge.

That I can imagine nothing more beautiful

than to propitiate such a god upon the seeds of my own heart.

SQUID

What could ever equal their quickening, their quicksilver jet pulse of
arrival and dispersal, mercurial purl and loop in the fluid arena of the
floodlight toward which they had been lured like moths to their un-
doing? We were eighteen that summer, Mike and I, working on an old
Greek-registered freighter carrying holds full of golden corn to Mexico,
corn that flowed like ancestral blood through the continent's veins and
south, down the aorta of the Mississippi, to be loaded for transport
across the Gulf. From Baton Rouge it was hours threading the delta
and one long night suspended between stars and the galaxies of lumi-
nescent plankton stirred up in our wake and then a week at anchor
awaiting a berth in the harbor at Veracruz. By the third day the sail-
ors had grown so restless the Captain agreed to lower the gangway as
a platform from which to fish for squid, which was not merely a meal
but a memento of home flashing like Ionian olive leaves. Ghost-eyed,
antediluvian, they darted upward, into the waiting, hand-held nets, and
then the sailors dropped everything to dash with their catch toward the
galley like grooms carrying brides to a nuptial bed, one slit to yank the
cartilage from white-purple flesh tossed without ceremony into a smok-
ing skillet, trickled with lemon and oil, a pinch of salt, and eaten barely
stilled, still tasting of the sea that had not yet registered its loss. That's
the image that comes back to me, the feast of the squid, and thereafter
we passed our evenings playing cards or ferried into port after a dinner
of oily moussaka by one of the ancient coal-burning tenders that made
the rounds like spark-belching taxis amongst the vessels lying at an-
chor, and the gargantuan rats drinking from the scuppers, and the leer-
ing prostitutes in the harbormaster's office, and the mango *batidos* Mike
preferred to beer, and the night we missed our ride back to the ship and

walked until the cafés closed and slept at the end of a long concrete breakwater, and the sky at first light a scroll of atoms, and the clouds at dawn as if drawn from a poem by Wallace Stevens, tinct of celadon and cinnabar and azure, and the locals waking on benches all around us, a whole neighborhood strolling out to squat and shit into the harbor, and then, piercing the clouds, aglow with sunlight for which the city still waited, the volcano—we'd never even guessed at its existence behind a mantle of perpetual mist—Pico de Orizaba, snow-topped Citlaltépetl like the sigil of a magus inked on vellum, and everything thereafter embellished by its hexwork, our lives forever stamped with that emblem of amazement, revelation, awe.

AN IRISH WORD

Canny has always been an Irish word
to my ear, so too its cousin *crafty*,
suggesting not only an appreciation of close-work,
fine-making, hand-wrought artistry,

but a highly evolved reliance on one's wits to survive,
stealth in the shadow of repressive institutions,
"silence, exile and cunning," in Joyce's admonition,
ferret-sly, fox-quick, silvery and elusive.

Craft, akin to *croft*—
a shepherd's crooked hawthorn staff,
wind-polished wolds and peat-spent moorlands
high in the Blue Stack Mountains.

Akin to *draught*—a pint of creamy stout
or a good stout draught horse
or a draughty old house
like the one in which my grandfather was born

near Drimnaherk, slate-roofed, hard-angled,
ringed by thistles in a soil-starved coomb.
His four brothers left home
bound for Australia, South Africa, Liverpool and Los Angeles

losing track of each other at once and forever
as if to loose the hawsers and set sail
were to sever every filial tether.
His name was Francis Daniel Campbell

but my grandmother Anna was a Monaghan
and her people had been
Maguires, Morans, Mohans, Meehans,
and other alliterative, slant-rhymed clans

all the way back to the nameless
bog-dwellers and kine folk.
When her father died suddenly in New York
he left three baby daughters and a widowed seamstress

with no recourse but retreat
to the old Rose Cottage overlooking Donegal Bay
in a parish of trellised thorns and ricked hay,
taking in mending and needlework to eat.

Market days they rode the train into Derry
to sell embroidered linens and hand-tatted lace,
kerchiefs monogrammed *z* to *a*.
She was nearing thirty

when she married and recrossed the Atlantic
and from her my own mother
had a recipe for soda bread, piles of drop-stitch
tablecloths, and a small stoneware pitcher

hand-painted in folksy script—
Be Canny Wi' the Cream.
Nothing could move my brother and I to screams
of laughter like that tiny pitcher,

so serious of purpose, so quaintly archaic,
as we slurped down bowls of Frosted Flakes
before school in the breakfast nook.
The scrupulous economy of the world it bespoke,

the frugality toward which it gestured,
were as inscrutable to us then
as the great sea cliffs at *Slieve League* when
we drove to the top at *Amharc Mór*

on a road so thickly fleeced with mist
we might have been lost if not for the sheep
materializing like guardian imps,
imperturbable creatures, black-faced ephreets,

the ocean one vast, invisible gong
struck by padded mallets or mailed fists.
Amharc Mór means "the grand view" in Irish
but all we saw was fog.

FOG

Driving down F_____ Avenue
on a foggy day in B_____,

the cabdriver, a Russian,
tips back his head at a stoplight

and falls fast asleep.
No car behind us, neon signs

muted, everything hushed, adrift.
After a moment I reach

to touch his shoulder and his eyes
slowly open. *Sorry,*

he says. *I was dreaming.*
And drives on.

NOTES ON THE POEM

1. The Foghorn

The poem one is writing is like a racehorse
running at a pace partially of one's choosing,
partially a function of conditions on the race course,
and partially determined by the horse's breeding.

But the poem one is about to start,
the poem one is going to write
immediately, very soon, perhaps next March,
is like a foghorn calling mournfully in the night.

If only the moon would concede its guilt
and come to heel like an obedient dog.
If only the horse could transform into a yacht.
If only the poet were a sailor, or fog.

2. The Vineyard

Like fraternal twins, like fated lovers, the poem and the life
of the culture intertwined: grafted vines
upthrust from ancient rootstocks in a vineyard
from whence issue blood oaths, drinking songs, and bloodred wine:
like that singing and its echo reflected inward,
mirror-dwellers, soul mates: hero and nemesis, man and wife.

3. The Poem

Maybe the poem will be strong as an ox
and carry us all the way home.

Maybe the poem will be small as a mole,
a field mouse hidden in a meadow.

Maybe the poem will sing like a whale.
Maybe the poem will turn into a frog when kissed.

Maybe it will be soft as mist.
Mysterious as fog. As white as snow.

The wind will blow but the poem
will not falter. It is solid as a rock.

Hard as ice. Fit as a fiddle.
True blue.

Maybe the poem will catch a chill,
take ill,

grow old and frail, fear death.
Maybe it will elude the hunters one more year,

but every poem draws a final—*inhale*—
breath.

4. *Wolves*

Often I feel as if I've forgotten how to write at all,
how to construct, or dream, or locate a poem,
and how, if found, to befriend it. Where are you, little poem?
Be careful, little poem, the forest is full of wolves.

But then I trace my way back, slowly, carefully,
as along an ocean cliff in the darkness,
treading barefoot on sandy stones and dune grass,
alone with the long, bitter moaning of the sea.

KINGDOM OF THE SEA MONKEYS

When I close my eyes the movie starts, the poem rises, the plot begins.

Falling asleep it comes to me, the novel I will never write, in semaphore flashes against my eyelids, flames from a torpedoed ship reflected on low clouds, flames abstract as green fingers, steam-machinery assembled from blueprints of another era, engine-gush of hot ash, a foliage of fears as lush as prehistoric ferns.

Up rises chaff from the threshing floor, up rises moon dust, city smoke, pulses of birdcall, voices chopped by wind into mews and phonemes.

The mind in the true dark at 3 A.M. when the electricity goes out with a bang—circling the ambit of consciousness, listening, probing, defending the perimeter, as long ago, fending off wolves with sharpened sticks when the fire died.

The perfecting of art, according to Kierkegaard, *is contingent upon the possibility of gradually detaching itself more and more from space and aiming toward time,*

a distinction analogous to that between perception and insight,

how the mind navigates like a bat, sometimes, soaring through its cavern via echolocation.

Other times it rests, perfectly still, like a bowl of pond water, a pure vessel in which the sediment, stirred up like flocks of swifts at dusk, swirls and drifts and settles, until its next disturbance, its next cyclonic effulgence.

Swirl, drift, settle.

It is the outside world that creates the self, that creates the sense of continuity on which the self depends—not the eyes, not the eyelash diffusing light, not the hands moving through the frame of observation, but the world.

We anchor ourselves within the familiar, like boats on an immensity of water.

Different day to day, yes—as the boardwalk of a town outside Genoa with its old carousel and honey-flavored ice-cream cones differs from a plain of sagebrush in Nevada—different and yet always and immediately recognizable. Ah, there it is again, the world. And so I too must still be here, within the container of myself, this body, this armature. As long as I can see out I can see in.

Therefore it is only through others that we know ourselves.

Therefore the limits of our compassion form the limits of our world.

Still our lives resemble dreams, luminous tapestries woven by a mechanism like the star machine at the planetarium, realms of fantastic desire and possibility, like the kingdom of the sea monkeys promised in the back pages of comic books of my childhood, the King of the Sea Monkeys with his crown and trident, his coral-hewn castle with pennants waving. That so much could be obtained for so little! And then the licking of postage stamps, and the mailing away, and the waiting.

Or perhaps it is less like a dream than a visionary journey,

to pilot the vehicle of consciousness through the turmoil of reality as if crossing the heart of a continent,

shadow of a hawk on asphalt clear as a photograph

as you rise from rich valleys into snowy mountains, black trees, meltwater, the striations of snow melting around the tree trunks like the growth rings within the wood of the trees themselves, layered accretions, historical pith.

Such a sad awakening it was, the day the sea monkeys arrived in the mail, no proud sea monarch or tiny mermaid minions, no castle, no scepter, no crown, just a little paper packet of dried brine shrimp which, tumbled into a fishbowl, resembled wriggling microscopic larvae, resembled sediment in pond water, swirling and drifting and settling.

Where is the King of the Sea Monkeys, the ruler of all memory?

Lost, and with him his kingdom, vanished like Atlantis beneath the waves, while we cling to life rafts and tea chests amid the flotsam, old movies projected like messages in bottles within the green-glass lyceums of our skulls.

Awakening, yes, as if startled from a dream.

As when, driving in heavy rain, you cross beneath an overpass and the world leaps with mystifying clarity at the windows of your eyes.

BALTIMORE

From the window, on a perfect August day, the great shade trees are unmoved, only the uncountable susurrations of their million-fold leaves betraying the breeze in its passage.

Roses in bloom, creepers climbing the porch railings, morning glory transforming the hedge into a vast, amorphous caterpillar of violet blossoms, some robins on the lawn hunting worms, two squirrels, an unabashed rabbit venturing out from its den within the ancient azalea bush.

The surface of the planet seethes with fellow creatures!

Their kinship touches a peculiar nerve, a spot not far from where art resides, primitive, cognizant of the animal nature of the species, the cave where Pan must once have lived, or still does.

And from the treetops the oceanic chorus of cicadas, described by Whitman as "rising and falling like brass quoits."

Specimen Days. As they all are. Wings pinned, chloroformed in glass vials,

catalogued for display in the dusty museum cases of time.

Chirp of some warbler, distant traffic, rumble of bass and drums from the all-day music festival at the racetrack where the teenagers in tie-dye and belly-button rings themselves resemble birds engaged in inscrutable mating rituals.

For blocks around concert-goers fill the streets, stoned or trippy on the day's sweet blue-sky vibe, little kids selling bottled water from red coolers, guys with knockoff sunglasses and T-shirts, the big grills set up on traffic islands for crab cakes and barbeque ribs.

The song the cicadas are singing they will sing throughout the brief weeks of their lives, exultant imagos mating in the high branches, and a new generation will emerge from freshly laid eggs, and burrow underground, ant-like grubs, wingless nymphs subsisting for the next seventeen years on fluids sucked from tree roots, with only that promise to help them endure their long, transitional dreamstate,

that memory or fragrance, a sunlit dance of green leaves in wind, that paradisal fragment of sensory data imprinted deep within their genes,

only that song—like quoits!—to lead them out of darkness.

CALIFORNIA LOVE SONG

To ride the Ferris wheel on a winter night in Santa Monica,
playing nostalgic songs on a Marine harmonica,
thinking about the past, thinking about everything
Los Angeles has ever meant to me, is that too much to ask?

To kiss on the calliope and uproot world tyranny
and strum a rhythm guitar Ron Wood would envy,
to long for the lost, to love what lasts, to sing
idolatrous praises to the stars, is that too much to ask?

Arm in arm to gallivant, to lark, to crow, to bask
in a wigwam of circus-colored atomic smog,
to quaff a plastic cup of nepenthean eggnog
over one more round of boardwalk Ski-ball,
to trade my ocean for a waterfall,
to live with you or not at all, is that too much to ask?

FIGURE FOR THE RECKLESS GRACE OF YOUTH

A tale from long ago—Ed riding his motorcycle
homeward at night along the freeways of Los Angeles
drunk and wearing only a pair of shorts and flip-flops,

and the next thing he knows being shaken awake
by a truck driver in a parking lot in Glendale
where he has slept like a babe far into the morning

on the grassy berm by a McDonald's drive thru window.
"Sorry to disturb you," the trucker says,
"but I didn't want the cops to take you in."

What is this a figure for,
an allegory of,
if not the reckless grace of youth?

Lightning-squall approaching off the ocean now,
giant, bulbous, white-grey cloud-mass
like titanic peonies glimpsed by strobe-light.

Then it arrives—window shades crashing, the house
full of wind as an owlet's skull,
and the flashes so close I shut my eyes

to their galvanic reiterations. No rain to speak of,
just the glittering electricity
of a fast-moving storm front passing through.

MINNEAPOLIS

Let's get drunk and drive someplace, way too fast and loving it. Let's get drunk and toss important stuff out the window—there goes the toaster, there goes a lamp. Let's get drunk and listen to the radiator hiss. Let's get drunk and go see the Replacements, already onstage and torching the amps with flamethrower guitars and Paul Westerberg's broken heart, oh gee whiz, worth living and dying for, worth working in salt mines or harvesting asteroids whose metallic cores might be smelted into alloys from which to fashion a robot able to invent a language in which we could speak of such music without diminishing it. Break. And after intermission they're so messed up they can hardly play "Unsatisfied" or even their ironically riveting versions of "Angel of the Morning" and TV theme songs and commercial jingles from childhood as we crowd forward on the dance floor shouting "Free Bird!" but Westerberg won't sing it, even when fifty people have taken up the chant, even as they're winding down, discordant, stumbling and complicit, and then a quick encore—"Left of the Dial"—honey-drenched, magnificent—before we're back out in the cold streets drinking cans of beer ensleeved in paper bags as so many are, were, and ever after shall be.

Surely this is the form and body of the world I have known,

entirely American,

and surely America's golden dreams shall yield to the sober and diminished light of dawn, all the bars of the Twin Cities arrayed like Nehi bottle caps on a checkered tablecloth, bars of the lost or damaged, bars of the utterly glorious in failure, pickled eggs and smeared lipstick, cornsilk and taxi-smoke over-flowing the gutters, the avenues and arteries,

a highway we think of as a river of molten tar,

wanting to get right down and bathe in it, partake of its stench and plen-itude, such is the nature of that grief, such the love for its wild aortal rush. And if you could harness all that, if you could mainline it or hook it to a turbine, you could power the world, you could live forever and rule the planet, you could flip the switch on the immensity we've created, jack up the volume on the damage we have wrought, blow the amps, fuck them all, every follicle, every corpuscle of their folly. Let the world eat the dust in the wake of our wicked ride, let them beg us for mercy, for succor or salvation, for the cuds of chaw or spent rifle shells we deign to bestow as they chase the shadows of our horses through empty streets, like the Mexican children at the end of the movie, calling out *Oye, Caballero, Mr. Cowboy, come back!*

GEORGE OPPEN

The way we live now, the larger portions
people are so delighted with,
new facilities, new buildings lost in sheen,
blurring the eyes to make
the synchronized fountains at the food court
resemble art.

More Hockney than Hopper
more Crane than Williams this

the new loneliness

the new con
formity

Consumer-colored clouds adrift
in a mall-colored sky as the movie-colored dusk
displaces the cautionary previews of sunset

and the stars emerge
self-conscious as adolescents modeling frosted lip gloss
in a window of bright merchandise,

numerous and alone.

THE FLY

As for the fly I chased around the bathroom with a towel that night,
    swatting, slapping, thrashing, pounding,
kicking with one foot the toothbrush cup onto its side, dislodging the
    tea curtain with a misplaced elbow,
unable for all my efforts to terminate his gallant loops and arabesques,
    his beeline dives and fighter-pilot vectorings,
his stalls and silences, his crafty retreats, his increasingly erratic bursts
    towards any open corner or avenue of escape,
behind the toilet, above the shower rod, inside the light wells,
    disappearing like a magician only to reappear again and again—
as for the fly, our struggle went on a long time. Too long. It was already
    after midnight when it began, the house calm,
everything dark beyond our gladiatorial arena, crazy to bother,
    ridiculous to carry on, but I was determined to finish it.

And when he stopped at last, gone for good, the body unseen but
    certainly dead, pulverized at a blow, squashed and unrecoverable,
when that silence was assured I felt certain of a conquest too small to
    call a triumph but a victory nonetheless.

And when, the next day, lifting a fresh towel from the bar, he fell to the
    floor, not dead but irreparably damaged,
lurching, toppling, lopsided, wing-still, no longer jittering with
    defiance, no longer challenging fate with desperate brio,
when I discovered him then everything had changed, and we were no
    longer fated to deadly opposition,

no longer entranced by the simplicity of our struggle, and I no longer
    understood the antagonism of the night before,
felt entirely alien from it, felt now that it was a perturbing frenzy, a
    kind of madness that had possessed me.

Which did not mean that he did not have to die, only that it was not, or
    not anymore, an act of murder but a cost of war,
or so I told myself, adorned in the common skin of my kind, naked
    before the mirror in the exalted light of morning.

DICK CHENEY SPEAKS TO ME IN A DREAM

The tree wells with sap, the sponge expands with brine,
a dishrag yields so much before it wrings dry,
it ends, it concludes, it terminates,
and you would tremble with fear to hear the briefings,
to see the demarcated targets—a certain fast-food restaurant
where the women resemble butchered turkeys
in running shoes and polyester pants, obese children
waving their sad little bologna arms—
this was a McDonald's in Ohio, I believe,
but I can't speak to that directly, I cannot stipulate,
Ohio or possibly Oklahoma, I do not recall the particulars,
or choose not to, an heuristic of blindness, if you will.
The point is this: these are the lame zebras,
the slow wildebeest at the watering hole,
and the judicious response is to cull the herd,
a calibrated rebalancing akin to natural selection,
which by no means contradicts intelligent design—
survival of the fittest is a free market paradigm.
And we have a full menu of implementation options,
amazing, some of the prototypes I've signed off on,
the know-how, the technology of this ordinance.
To reflect honestly, I am awed at our place in the schema,
I am awed at the nimbus, almost a translucency,
the light shining right through solid objects.
We have so much to be thankful for and the prisoner
wants to take that from us but he will talk,
and when he does we will have the right team in place,

the appropriate people to make sense of his jabbering,
officers and specialists, magnificently trained,
folks who have dedicated their entire lives to this pursuit.
Freedom is a tough monkey but we will make him sing.

VICE PRESIDENT OF PANTS

turns out to be my friend Marvin's job title
at a local clothing manufacturer
as I learned from a recent newspaper article
about "victims of the downturn,"

though even after some serious erosion
his paycheck rolls enough biweekly zeroes
to belie whatever expectations
you may have harbored about those

who toil in the vineyards of leisure wear,
and I can't help but envy the Director of Kneesocks,
and the Under-Secretary of Ascots,
and wonder whether the *Alcalde of Guayaberas*

might be hiring an assistant sometime soon,
because in all honesty this poetry gig
is like feeding chocolate donuts to a hungry tiger
or planting sunflowers on the moon.

Yes, the darkness is vast and it surrounds us. Our lives compose slim
  chapters of clarity bookended by the void.
Islanded within ourselves we slide across the surface of the infinite like
  icebergs adrift on unplumbable waters,
and even to scale our own consciousness we must hack a ladder of
  footholds into a wall of shimmering blue ice
with the very words that fail us precisely when we come to speak of
  what underlies that scintillant Arctic sea.
And, yes, humility is a profound and appropriate response in the face of
  the unknown, the intuited, the envisioned but unseen.
We have all been moved by strange auroras in the night skies of our
  grief, felt ourselves lifted upon geysers of spiritual yearning,
desires inchoate as embryonic galaxies, forces so powerful we cry out to
  understand them and so to understand ourselves.
Because understanding flows from and back toward knowledge, from
  deep thought, contemplative analysis,
from the thirst for comprehension by which to order our lives toward
  some coherent mold, some habitable form.
Knowledge gives shape to the streaming flux of existence like a magnet
  beneath a table of iron filings.
Knowledge is a beacon at the edge of the fog-bound ocean as well as the
  vessels we sail in, ark and carrack and coracle
alike constructed in accordance with our needs and abilities and the
  limits to the human capacity for sense-making.
The mind resembles a lighthouse, then, a hearth for thought's flame, as
  much as it does a temple to magnetism or pure fire.

The mind is a complex, many-chambered organ, stone-hungry and
ruminative, like the stomach of an elk.
Like the heart it may atrophy, like the liver it regenerates, like the skin it
serves both to shelter and imprison.
The mind resembles an amoeba shuddering with Brownian motion,
vibrating its sensory apparatus against a disinterested world,
but unlike that organism it must record its data in the brain's
repository of scrolls and inscribed wax cylinders,
a process fraught with mystery, imprecision, difficulty and loss, because
the means of transcription is the flawed stylus of language.
Language is like the tool-kit of a gem-cutter: it offers a dazzlingly fine
but finite array of chisels and gimlets, augers and saws,
it can only enhance the diamond's inherent flame, only edge and bevel
what is held against its blade.
Yet to spend one's time decrying its limitations is both futile and
petulant, while choosing to use it arbitrarily,
to inscribe graffiti on the plexiglass panels of a phone booth, say, may
be funny but remains sophomoric, and ultimately meaningless.
And for a poet to forsake meaning within language is like a high tower
aerialist in the midst of a swan-dive towards that turquoise pool
deciding to crash like a kamikaze instead because the water appears
murky, inadequate and historically-determined.
Yes, the parable of the high-diver is subject to alternative
interpretations—renunciation of the familiar may be a virtue
though alteriority is not in and of itself a moral triumph—and, yes, the
metaphor of the gem-cutter is imprecise,

the world is more granite than tiger's eye opal, we must quarry cobbles
    to pave with and cornerstones to build upon—
language is not a form of knowledge (the child stung by a bee needs no
    word to understand pain) but an agent of its transmission,
a specialized, species-specific mode of communication, a socially-
    constructed operating system, a semiotically-interactive meta-archive.
And, yes, all archives are full of redundant volumes, so many slates
    over-written to erase outdated truths.
But knowledge, like language, is organically adaptive; it is not a field of
    eroded gravestones but a sheaf of palimpsests,
not a destination but a voyage of Odyssean perils—consider the science
    of Aryan supremacy, or how the conquering Mexica
commenced the Aztec hegemony by burning their codices and
    fabricating a history more appropriate to their glory.
Nor are the fruits of knowledge innocent of risk, so many rueful Fausts
    and Oppenheimers marinating in regret.
Knowledge is replete with shibboleths and false gods: let us
    acknowledge the solipsistic lure of pure intellect,
the egotistical oyster around the pearl of the idea, the self-perpetuating
    think tanks and robotics labs of ideology.
Sometimes knowledge and ignorance seem like horses galloping
    cinematically across a sagebrush plateau
dragging the stagecoach of humanity ever closer to the abyss—but it is
    naïve or nihilistic to declare their contest a race between equals,
and we must acknowledge the moral and ethical consequences of which
    animal we choose to place our bets upon.

And if our lives, to large degree, are a calculus of such decisions, then
the mechanism of their resolution must be the abacus of knowledge.
Are we merely accountants, then, button pushers, existential
technocrats? No, for knowledge is fluid, multiform, polyvalent—
taxonomists of butterflies and molecular chemists may live without
cognizance of generative phonology—
knowledge incorporates self-limitation, it admits lacunae and accepts
error even as it seeks to extend its dominion.
Are we intellectual imperialists, therefore, who assay and conquer on its
behalf? If we carry the natives away in chains, yes,
if we set fire to their villages and privatize their resources, if hubris
overwhelms empathy and common sense.
But self-criticism is itself an essential form of knowledge: the
recognition of past mistakes and the resolution to avoid their
repetition.
Let us so resolve: if there must be an earthly polity let it be the kingdom
of knowledge, the empire of empirical inquiry,
founded upon the obdurate task of understanding, built by the labor of
brows creased in earnest contemplation.
And what of the untold mysteries beyond our ken, what of the blind
enveloping void of the universe, for the darkness is vast, the
darkness surrounds us?
Let us abrogate its dire prerogative. Let us diminish the compass of its
terrestrial sway. Let us turn on the lights and say *good night*.

THE MOUNTAIN

One could live on the mountain for many years, a lifetime, an age of men, seeing only the face of the world selected by the Director—the ancient forest, chestnut and beech yielding to pines and the rocky barren peaks retreating, eventually, to snow-clad fastnesses, and the deep contemplative thrust of sunlight through young leaves, and the old terraces stair-stepping the mountainside no longer cultivated efficiently, olive and lemon groves run wild with brambles, and the slate rooftops of the farmhouse and outbuildings held down with fieldstones, and a single cow walking past as if to mock the scale of the local wildlife—toad, scorpion, bat, cat—and an old man who has pulled his car to the side of the road to stand precariously on a wall at the cliff's edge waving a long, wiggly stick overhead in pursuit of wild cherries, and the six types of fruit trees on the terrace below—fig, plum, peach, apple, apricot, lemon—figs like sows' ears discarding their seeds by moonlight and lemons too fragrant, too glorious for words,

and rosemary and thyme and mint but no basil,

and lanes of oleander and cascading roses, the pink roses torn, overblown, funereal—no, but sad and tattered,

like abandoned bridal bouquets,

while the red roses burst forth in erotic profusion,

and the young green shoots of the pruned grapevines ascending madly from their trellises, striving for vindication, for consummation, finding only the cool, mineral air, or the prop of a fellow aspirant, lover or brother, prop with which to intertwine and reach again toward the unyielding sky,

and the little meadow where the grasses rise to mid-thigh, and thorny creepers dart across the path, and the trickle of the brook as it tumbles down the slope, the meadow that does not forbid entrance though it does not invite it, where the pear tree stands black and wizened as a crone, where the ground grows marshy with runoff in the spring, the seldom-entered meadow,

and the bark of a dog to bring the silence into focus,

and a breeze, smelling of dust and lavender, bearing occasional news from the sea,

and precisely six lights at night—four from the hamlet in the valley where the silvery river tumbles over rocks, another from the town on the next hillside where the church bell rings once every hour—sometimes twice, at five before and then, as if issuing a correction, at the stroke of the actual hour—and a mysterious sixth light, on a ridge across the valley, origin unknown,

and nasturtiums and euphorbia and stands of red zinnias in bloom, coming to bloom, alongside hydrangea, hollyhocks, phlox, orange poppies, tiny daisies white and purple, wildflowers of all sorts, the aforementioned roses, and bugs of all kinds, spiders, crickets, the lavender beds abuzz with wasps and fuzzy bumblebees, and huge hornet-like creatures with curved proboscises pollinating the globes of allium, and the small flitting butterflies, one species blue with pale spots, the other yellow-gold with black, and moths, and metallic beetles, silver and turquoise, and the fireflies which rise out of the heavy grass at sunset and turn off, simultaneously, at dusk, and the hopping bugs of many sorts, and the flying bugs foolish enough to discover a flower in a human ear, and a multitude of ants crawling everywhere, ants like automata sent forth from the machine-works deep within the mountain, sent forth by the Director, no doubt, but for what purpose, to what unfathomable end?

SNAKE RIVER, END OF MARCH

Near-silence along the swirling, pearl-green Snake River, steady tread of footfalls on the path, electric lines from the downstream dam conducting a discourse of power through the canyon and away without a sound. Goose shit along the trail, barest blush of wild carrot, flowers like baby asters rising out of a grayish, alpine moss. Once or twice I startle geese from the bank—they rise up, bellicose, and splash down mid-stream, honks of annoyance drifting swiftly westward on the river's chalky, mineral-rich flow. The tide laps quietly, like a mouse sipping milk from a teaspoon, and I feel, so far away from my family, dazzlingly alone, like an Inca mourning his vanished civilization. These hills resemble Irish mountains in their sculptural grace, their treeless amplitude, their saurian greens and shale browns and straw-colored bands of broom, and where they have been tilled the soil shimmers dark as unrefined chocolate, spring wheat inching sunward to dye them the color of waxed grocery-store limes. They are so steep! The cows appear ant-sized, sure-footed as llamas clinging to sinuous, sun-rippled slopes. The winding country road across the Palouse and down to this canyon would be a highway in Ireland, or the Andes, though the nearest town is nothing but silos and crane gantries to load the river barges with barley. From here you can float all the way to the Pacific Ocean, past apple orchards and salmon ladders, locks and spillways, drowsy horses in winter blankets near a gully painted yellow by swaths of early-blooming daffodils. After a while I climb back to the gravel parking lot and sit at a green picnic table beside my rented Pontiac. Charred remains of hot dogs, a half-eaten lollipop in the grass, sound of songbirds, sporadic hammering—a ranger is repairing the roofs of the picnic pavilions up the road. Otherwise, silence, or nearly. Water slapping riverstones, calm propulsion of heart and lungs, ageless hills like the musculature of buried giants emerging from winter. O broken, the becoming, the becoming—.

ALBUQUERQUE

5:30 A.M. at the Holiday Inn Express outside Albuquerque, New Mexico,
listening to Neil Young singing "Albuquerque,"
a song like unruly silver smoke coiled across an autumn sky.

At the desk I drink my black tea, eating slices of blood orange,
watching heavy snow settle across the parking lot
like volcanic ruin upon Pompeii,

the ash-fall of human suffering,
an ether in which we are jarred and preserved
like fetuses afloat in formaldehyde.

Last night, coming down from Santa Fe, moon rising
triumphant over tiers of snowy mountains,
variegated textures of the tree-cover and the naked peaks,

snow fields capturing variably tinted angles of reflection,
raw silver or titanium blue,
the highest altitudes skeletal as ivory,

like sugar skulls lit by processional torches,
startled, deer-eyed, ore-like light
beneath fast-scudding clouds the color of icebergs,

indigo plains running away to the south and west,
white wave-crests of the distant ranges,
and the road a thin whistle in deep silence.

No, it was tonight—another day
but this same night, almost past, almost dawn,
but not quite.

Snow is lessening, and even here, in scrubland near the airport,
there are peaks like rough buffalo humps,
rocky flanks screened by clouds and evergreens.

How prodigiously important it all seems,
how profound and vital,
the inscrutable message of moonlight on mountains,

the message of the night,
which is planetary and elemental,
message of the blizzard, which I cannot decipher,

the message in a song to which I am listening very, very carefully,
spitting seeds into a plastic cup,
waiting for morning, or a break in the storm.

NIGHTS ON PLANET EARTH

Heaven was originally precisely that: the starry sky, dating back to the earliest Egyptian texts, which include magic spells that enable the soul to be sewn in the body of the great mother, Nut, literally "night," like the seed of a plant, which is also a jewel and a star. The Greek Elysian fields derive from the same celestial topography: the Egyptian "Field of Rushes," the eastern stars at dawn where the soul goes to be purified. That there is another, mirror world, a world of light, and that this world is simply the sky—and a step further, the breath of the sky, the weather, the very air—is a formative belief of great antiquity that has continued to the present day with the godhead becoming brightness itself: *dios/theos* (Greek); *deus/divine/Diana* (Latin); *devas* (Sanskrit); *daha* (Arabic); *day* (English).

—SUSAN BRIND MORROW, *WOLVES AND HONEY*

1.

Gravel paths on hillsides amid moon-drawn vineyards,
click of pearls upon a polished nightstand
soft as rainwater, self-minded stars, oboe music
distant as the grinding of icebergs against the hull
of the self and the soul in the darkness
chanting to the ecstatic chance of existence.
Deep is the water and long is the moonlight
inscribing addresses in quicksilver ink,
building the staircase a lover forever pauses upon.
Deep is the darkness and long is the night,
solid the water and liquid the light. How strange
that they arrive at all, nights on planet earth.

2.

Sometimes, not often but repeatedly, the past invades my dreams in the
form of a familiar neighborhood I can no longer locate,
a warren of streets lined with dark cafés and unforgettable bars, a place
where I can sing by heart every song on every jukebox,
a city that feels the way the skin of an octopus looks pulse-changing
from color to color, laminar and fluid and electric,
a city of shadow-draped churches, of busses on dim avenues, or
riverlights, or canyonlands, but always a city, and wonderful, and
lost.
Sometimes it resembles Amsterdam, students from the ballet school
like fanciful gazelles shooting pool in pink tights and soft,
shapeless sweaters,
or Madrid at 4 A.M., arguing the *18th Brumaire* with angry Marxists, or
Manhattan when the snowfall crowns every trash-can king of its
Bowery stoop,
or Chicago, or Dublin, or some ideal city of the imagination, as in a
movie you can neither remember entirely nor completely forget,
barracuda-faced men drinking sake like yakuza in a Murakami novel,
women sipping champagne or arrack, the rattle of beaded curtains
in the back,
the necklaces of Christmas lights reflected in raindrops on windows,
the taste of peanuts and their shells crushed to powder underfoot,
always real, always elusive, always a city, and wonderful, and lost. All
night I wander alone, searching in vain for the irretrievable.

3.

In the night I will drink from a cup of ashes and yellow paint.
In the night I will gossip with the clouds and grow strong.
In the night I will cross rooftops to watch the sea tremble in a dream.
In the night I will assemble my army of golden carpenter ants.
In the night I will walk the towpath among satellites and cosmic dust.
In the night I will cry to the roots of potted plants in empty offices.
In the night I will gather the feathers of pigeons in a honey-jar.
In the night I will become an infant before your flag.

SUGAR OR BLOOD

In the kitchen Elizabeth has been making marmalade
with the luxurious crop of our lemon tree,
and from my desk I can almost taste the caramelizing essence
of citrus rind and vanilla beans and burnt sugar,
and I can hear the piano concerto by Mozart she is listening to,
which sounds like a pavilion constructed from lemon-tinted panes of
    sugar-glass,
and the Zairean music I'm listening to is like a tessellated and
    betasseled tapestry
thrown upon the floor of a nomad's tent, and the sands of the Sahara
continue their migration into the timeworn grasslands of the Sahel,
and the Virunga volcanoes comprise a fog-shouldered heaven
to the last families of mountain gorillas awaking before dawn,
shy, Herculean versions of ourselves, brothers
from a simpler dream, luminous and transient as meteors.
There will come no more into this world
when we have killed the last of them. So many
spools of golden sorrow to unwind,
so much pathos to weave upon a loom of human agency.
As if we were not ourselves baboons on the savannah,
not jackals, not giraffes in our ungainliness.
As if to desire the coat of a jaguar, the fur of a snow leopard,
was not a form of worship, as raw ore minted and coined
resembles the child's flattering imitation of a mastery it will never
    equal.
Who would not be a great cat in the Amazon or the Hindu Kush?
Even the greenish pelt of a river monkey, its iridescent aura,

even our too-human bodies shimmer with the weird, atomic eclipse-
    light of life.
Talking to myself like this, in a blazon and an emblem,
I realize I have never said plainly most of what I truly believe,
I have shied from difficulty and misstated my deepest fears,
I have not borne full witness to the suffering in the streets of the cities
    I love,
I have not walked a picket line against the tyranny of greed,
I have been wily and evasive even on behalf of art,
I have not praised the movies in tones equal to the rapture
I have known there,
I cannot remember *King Lear,*
I did not finish *Ulysses* or even start on Proust,
even now I seek diversion in the candy necklace of delight,
even now I refuse to commit,
even now I would walk among jaguars
wearing the skin of a jaguar
as if it were not necessary to declare my allegiance,
as if I did not have to choose.
Which will it be, sugar or blood?

II

THE CUSTODIAN

1.

My old friend John stops by for a few days on his way to visit his older brother, dying of cancer in Tampa. Twenty years since we drank a bottle of cheap scotch together on 105th Street, talking all night about books and their power to transform the world, talking about poetry as if it might save us from the darkness. These days, we agree, there are no simple answers to be found in that bottle, though it is not the worst place to look. For over a decade John has worked as a custodian at a university in California, mopping the corridors of quiet buildings, talking with the young professors, working for the union, carrying a ring of keys to unlock darkened laboratories and libraries. He has discovered amazing things in the book stacks in the small hours of the night, hand-printed pamphlets from Mayakovsky, the plays of Sadakichi Hartmann, untranslated poems of Roberto Bolaño. Sometimes poets famous for their political commitment come to read on campus and he alone knows that the kitchen workers in that particular building are bullied and abused by a notorious boss, but they, the workers, immigrants from Laos and El Salvador, refuse to file union grievances, refuse to confront authority in any fashion, too familiar in their previous lives with its costs. That's my niche, he says, between the poets and the dishwashers. Not to bring them together but simply to bridge the distance, the space between lives and words, the passion of the mind to connect and the intransigence of the world restraining it.

2.

For lunch we go to a Peruvian restaurant in the city and eat ceviche of mussels and onions and a platter of fried shrimp and octopus with bottles of Cristál beer.

He would like to live in Cuzco or Lima, find a way to visit Nicanor Parra in Chile.

He would like to live in Mexico City for a while and translate young poets back and forth across that frontier.

For a couple years I trained to be a masseur, he says, at an institute run by a Japanese master, and one day I felt against my palm a pulse of wind rising from a woman's back as surely as I feel the wind on my face right now—I was looking around the room for the draft, as if it were a practical joke, but it was what it was—pure energy rising out of the body.

Why did you give it up? I ask.

People would say, *You saved my life!*—and they would mean it. I didn't want to be that person. I don't believe in saviors.

3.

The last night of his visit we sat up late talking in the backyard, John smoking his unfiltered cigarettes, our bodies marked by the passage of time but our minds still turning familiar gears, still worrying the old bones—as if the years were the transcript of a trial we could review at command, as if the mind is a prisoner and the thread of its movement restlessly pacing the corridors of a decaying labyrinth might even now be rewound and reexamined.

Consciousness is a caged tiger, John said, raging against the bars.

But the capsules of our minds open so infrequently, I said, like the air-locks on some giant spaceship. We could live together like penguins, like ants, we could be bees in a hive and still not know each other.

A tree frog sat with us, balled on the windowsill, pale and wide-eyed, like a glob of uncooked pastry dough, as the winter trade winds flung the leaves of the live oak tree down upon our heads like soft axe-blows, talking about translation and semiotics and novels written on cell phones by green-haired teenagers in Tokyo subway stations, argu-ing about literature and how it evolves, or degrades, or transforms—does anyone still read Zbigniew Herbert the way we did, or Delmore Schwartz, or Malcolm Lowry, does anyone care about Huidobro, Tran-strömer, Pessoa?—eulogizing great bookstores and the evanescence of artifacts, the long-prophesied death of the book, quotidian relic of an archaic technology.

But books have been my whole life, he said. What will we do without them?

Loneliness is everywhere, John. Not even poetry can save us.

ALLEN GINSBERG

I met him only once, at a party in Vinnie Katz's old apartment above a
  Thai restaurant on 55th Street in Chicago, spring of 1983 or '84.
Earlier that evening he gave a reading at the university, finger cymbals,
  ashram chanting, not as much of the early ecstatic genius as had
  been hoped,
not the majestic anguish of "Howl" but a serious performance
  nonetheless, warmly greeted by an audience of many hundreds.
It seemed even more crowded at the party, where Vinnie's band, The
  Throbbers, a loose-jointed, Velvets-inspired power trio,
rattled the walls of the linoleum-tiled kitchen as we did our usual
  thing, menthol cigarettes and aggressive dancing,
cheap liquor sloshed from aluminum ashtrays, a lot of ironic social
  commentary on secondhand couches smelling of smoke and cat piss.
Ginsberg sat hunched in a back room, buddha-like, holding court; the
  omnisexual dimension of his Socratic shtick was a bit unnerving,
even worse was the way Peter Orlovsky would flick the tip of my nose
  with his finger as I posed burning questions like, *Why did Kerouac
  have to die, man?*
He seemed tired, sure, how many times had he been through this
  routine, how many earnest young poets dreaming of glory,
looking for wisdom or validation or whatever, how many dim
  bohemian scenes edging toward ash-blistered dawn,
but his patience never faltered, his tipsy smile, he never sold out the
  night or the life or the art that counted him as a bead on its prayer-
  string.
And then it was dawn, or something like it, near dawn, Chicago—
  though it could have been New York, Denver, San Francisco,

the American city in all its splendid yearning to be lost and longing to
   belong, its sidewalks of dog shit and sparkling mica,
a train passing over the viaduct, the embankment spectral with waif-
   paper and what I took to be ghost-weeds trembling in the vinegar
   light.
Not weeds but coarse flowers risen from the pavement. Not ghosts but
   souls seeking voices to greet the dawn.

TWO POEMS FOR FRANK O'HARA

1.

Tonight the clouds resemble French surrealists
soft and electric and hot to the touch
hustling north from the New York Public Library
as if to grab the lease of the vacant apartment on E. 49th Street
Frank O'Hara rented for $31 a month in 1952.

Poor clouds. They have no sense of time

and no one has told them about the market system
and, being French, the plane trees in Bryant Park
have filled their beautiful heads
with a lightning storm of longing for Paree.

2.

The School of O'Hara was like the School of Hard Knocks
only less so a school of tickles a school of muffled taps
a school of mittened hands at the piano assaying Rachmaninoff.
All in all Frank was a pretty good teacher he mostly taught
geometry mostly because of his fondness for Pi.
What could be more beautiful than Pi he often said to us
his faithful students who loved him dearly and not least
for a cognac stain in the shape of Delaware Bay on his collar
clearly visible in the light through the windows he threw open
those mornings to the cool clatter of city busses
and the pomp of geraniums potted in rusty coffee cans
o! what could be more ruthless and beautiful and true
than a science built upon an indeterminable constant?

THE READING SERIES

We had come back that year to Chicago from New York,
living on the North Side three blocks from Wrigley Field,
and I was apprenticed as an adjunct wage-slave
hither and yon at sundry colleges across Chicagoland,
while Elizabeth caught the El to the Loop each morning
to work as a graphic designer with her aunt,
pasting together advertising circulars for power tools at Sears,
and I wanted to keep involved, to mimic some fraction
of the literary doings we'd known in Manhattan,
and so called up an old friend who managed a bookstore
and offered to run a reading series for him. It was nothing
too spectacular. We'd bring in local poets of various factions,
old friends come to visit, people passing through town
whose work came highly recommended,
anyone willing to read for fifty bucks and the chance
to sell a dozen books, and who, in those days,
desired anything more? I'm no longer certain precisely
who read for us, whether Yusef Komunyakaa
drove up from Indiana or if that was later, and elsewhere,
but I remember Li-Young Lee, Luis Rodriguez,
David Wojahn and Lynda Hull, the time Dean Young
turned metalinguistic handstands in his desperation
to evoke any response at all from the six or seven
recalcitrant catatonics who had wandered in to listen
in lieu of the enthusiastic crowd I had promised
and we had some pitchers of beer afterwards at Jimmy's
and pondered the futility and injustice of our lives.

So much has changed since then it's hard to recover
the sense of urgency and risk that swirled about those days
like tornadoes of cigarette smoke in a South Side taproom.
Which is another 20th Century peril laid to rest:
the chance of death from tobacco at one remove.
Not that I begrudge it or would look the gift horse
of these last two glittering decades in the kisser.
Why not, as Flaubert suggests, live a more common life
and save one's madness for the unruled page?
Not that I advocate insanity of any stripe, but it is better
to domesticate the tiger than to be devoured by it.
Yet despite their stereotype as a caste of oddballs,
troubled souls and psychic yoyos, most poets nowadays
sport designer eyewear and can maintain
polite conversation with little or no drooling.
The problem is that the exceptions are so egregiously
self-aggrandizing as to condemn the long-suffering majority
to dwell in the shadows of their gargantuan neuroses—
think toxic sycophancy overlaid with Francophilia,
germ phobia combined with predatory philandering,
rampant elitism on a bed of Earth Mother greens.
To this day the most unabashedly narcissistic person
I have ever encountered remains a turtle-necked poet
who graced our reading series with his presence that year,
a man who was to vanity as the ostrich is
to flightlessness and eggs. Indeed, the shell of his ego
was so perfectly formed it shone like a pearl, and its embryo

no doubt would be the first of its kind to fly.
He began by describing in detail his youthful training
at a Midwestern state university, listing alphabetically
his teachers and peers, names I struggled to place
but he, mistaking my confusion for admiration, said:
"Yes, it was the Golden Age of poetry in Missouri."
Or Ohio, or Wisconsin, I forget—though he most certainly
played some vital part in those golden ages, too.
"You could say," he said, "that in those days
I was the Great White Hope of poetry, the next big thing."
He smiled at the memory, and we smiled with him,
partly out of reflex politeness, partly from mortification,
but also because it was impossible not to admire
the radiant purity of his self-absorption,
the Shakespearean grandeur of his self-regard,
as he told his astonishing tales not in the brash tones
of a braggart or a raconteur, but raptly and sincerely,
sure of the delight his words must inevitably spread,
like a kid sharing out bubble gum the day after Halloween.
Such as this one time he was invited to read
before the Union of People's Writers or some such
august assembly deep in the old Soviet bloc,
and the audience, no less than twenty thousand strong,
rose as one to applaud as he emerged onstage,
and he turned to his translator to ask:
"But, Sergei, who are they applauding for?"
And the answer was: "For you, my friend—for you!

You are a hero to every writer in Bulgaria!"
Or Moldova, or Turkmenistan, or wherever.
And that was it, the whole story. You kept waiting
for the other shoe to drop but it was just the one shoe,
all by its lonesome, the sound of one shoe clapping,
or simply wagging its tongue with joy for its master.
And still I could not find it in myself to look askance,
or stop myself from merrily nodding along
as he segued into the saga of his triumphant wooing
of Hollywood starlets even while struggling
to pick up a grizzled cocktail waitress at the hotel bar,
she signifying the depth of her disinterest
by yawning dramatically while spilling change from her tray
in a silver cataract across our table and onto the floor.
This all took place before the reading.
It was autumn, and raining, and our days in Chicago
were numbered, though we didn't know it then.
Elizabeth was four months pregnant
and we had etched constellations on the pantry ceiling
and tacked down a carpet the color of buttered popcorn
to create a sparrow-sized nursery for the baby
we could not yet imagine to be Sam.
It was always raining, in my memory, those nights
of the reading series at the bookstore in Hyde Park.
Or snowing, or pelting down sleet, or the air aswim
with fog or falling leaves or pink and white petals storming
from the branches of some late-flowering ornamental.

Between poems I could see Elizabeth nodding off—
it was hot in the room, the baby made her so tired—
and we slipped outside for a breath of air as the great man
told again the story of the marvelous reading in Russia.
Looking back through the rain-puzzled window
as he worked the crowd of a dozen damp, incurious souls
slumped in metal folding chairs, each, to his vision,
an adoring fan, I said: "Think of it this way—
with that big turnout in Stalingrad, and this bunch tonight,
he's still averaging more than ten thousand a show."
Elizabeth smiled, eyelashes jeweled with mist,
and placed my hand upon the globe of her stomach.
"Yes," she said. "But we all want to be loved."

NOTES ON COMPRESSION

Expansiveness and compression are not binary opposites but two sides
    of a coin from which all poetry can profit.
What sense to tell Whitman to compress his poems into Dickinson's
    reeling, divinatory, off-kilter stanzas?
Walt contains ecstatic multitudes, Emily contains mute multitudes,
    heads of pins contain angelic multitudes.
The point is not the manner of the multitude but the size of the
    ballroom and the type of music to which they dance.

•

Compression, like the weed whacker,
is not a fit tool for every occasion.

•

A picture is worth a thousand words.

So images are not only vehicles of compression
but complex financial transactions
on the stock exchange of symbolic cognition.

Why spend a million bucks
when four letters buys you the moon?

•

:)

•

A simile is simply an equal sign,
a coupling-device in a linguistic equation.

thou = summer day

But a metaphor is an atomic bomb,
every flower, city, wineglass,
wood stork and raindrop in the entire world
contained in the wobbling, unstable nucleus
of a single atom of uranium. And then—.

•

$e = mc^2$

•

Poetry often resembles those little capsules
you buy at the Dollar Store
for the kids to play with in the bathtub—

drop one into the warm water of consciousness
and it blossoms into a seahorse,

a dragon, a tiny elephant made of sponge.

•

cmprsn!

•

When a friend asked me to contribute to a collection of micro-essays on poetic craft, two or three hundred words, no more than a couple paragraphs, I knew the exact topic I wanted and told her my essay would be called "Compression," and when it reached eleven pages with no end in sight I called back to say never mind.

POETRY AND THE WORLD

In the world of some poets
there are no Cheerios or Pop-Tarts, no hot dogs
tumbling purgatorially on greasy rollers,
only chestnuts and pomegranates,
the smell of freshly baked bread,
summer vegetables in red wine, simmering.

In the world of some poets
lucid stars illumine lovers
waltzing with long-necked swans in fields
flush with wildflowers and waving grasses,

there are no windowless classrooms,
no bare, dangling bulbs,
no anxious corridors of fluorescent tubes.

In the world of some poets
there is no money and no need
to earn it, no health insurance,
no green cards, no unceremonious toil.

And how can we believe in that world
when the man who must clean up after the reading
waits impatiently outside the door
in his putty-colored service uniform,
and the cubes of cheese at the reception
taste like ashes licked from a bicycle chain,

when the desk-tops and mostly-empty seats
have been inscribed with gutter syllabics
by ballpoint pens gripped tight as chisels,
and the few remaining students are green
as convalescents narcotized by apathy?

But—that's alright. Poetry
can handle it.

Poetry is a capacious vessel, with no limits
to its plasticity, no end to the thoughts and feelings
it can accommodate,
no restrictions upon the imaginings
it can bend through language into being.

Poetry is not the world.
We cannot breathe its atmosphere,
we cannot live there, but we can visit,
like sponge divers in bulbous copper helmets
come to claim some small portion
of the miraculous.

And when we leave we must remember
not to surface too rapidly,
to turn off the lights in the auditorium
and lock the office door—there have been thefts
at the university in recent weeks.

We must remember not to take the bridge
still under construction, always under construction,

to stop on the causeway for gas

and pick up a pack of gum at the register,
and a bottle of water,
and a little sack of plantain chips,

their salt a kind of poem, driving home.

A SHORT GUIDE TO POETIC FORMS

1. Villanelle

Bouncing along like a punch-drunk bell,
its Provençal shoes too tight for English feet,
the villanelle is a form from hell.

Balletic as a tapir, strong as a gazelle,
strict rhyme and formal meter keep a beat
as tiresome as a punch-drunk bell-

hop talking hip hop at the IHOP—*no substitutions
on menu items, no fries with the chimichanga,
no extra syrup*—what the hell

was that? Where did my rhyme go—uh, compel—
almost missed it again, damn, can you feel the heat
coming off this sucker? Red hot! *Ding!* (Sound of a bell.)

Hey, do I look like a busboy to you, like an el-
evator operator, like a trained monkey or a parakeet
singing in my cage? Get the hell

out of the Poetry Hotel!
defeat   mesquite   tis mete   repeat
Bouncing along like a punch-drunk bell,
the villanelle is a form from—*Write* it!—hell.

2. *Faulty Ghazal*

I remember the mountain poppy, scent of jasmine and flowering basil.
There is only one culture, crying for the mud of its origin.

All the courtesans in Islamabad were named Roxanne.
One word in the stanza to repeat, one wind in the reeds along the lake.

If the mole hunts the cricket, what does the mole-cricket hunt?
Thirst, flour, moon, turtle, mirror, magnet, Campbell.

To traffic in the heart of the volcano, remember your asbestos gloves,
    Campbell.
Idols etched in sandstone have no fear of the apocalypse, Campbell.

No trick for Campbell to walk in the forest by night:
wisdom is asleep and will not trouble him.

3. N + 7

What's up with these new, postmodern, randomizer-type forms
where you employ computers to generate all the text,
or you steal (the preferred verb is: *appropriate*) the text
from some government report or Gothic novel or equally antique form
of literature and then scissor sentences from odd-numbered pages
to fall like snowflakes onto your blank, white page.

And that's the poem, a chance-enacted word-blizzard.
In the "N + 7" form you take a sentence and mark the nouns—
"kiss my (*blister*)," for example—and then go to the dictionary
(so tweedy and traditional, that crazy old dictionary)
and find the seventh noun in sequence after the subject noun,
and substitute it. And so we get: "kiss my (*blizzard*)."

Before hatching out your own batch of N + 7 lines
practice noun-substitution with these sample lines.

"(*Art*) is not an (*accident*)."
"The (*arbitrary*) is the (*enemy*) of (*creativity*)."
"Please take your (*foolish games*) and go back to (*France*)."

4. *Sonnets for Beginners*

I

Sonnet, in Italian, means "little room,"
while a *sonnet crown* is not a hat but a sequence
of interlinked sonnets, i.e., "rooms,"
elegantly connected to resemble, in a sense,

a stylish suite at the Rome Hilton,
or maybe a nice-sized apartment—
that would be *appartamento* in Italian—
yes, a comfortable, high-ceilinged apartment,

with plenty of morning sun, not too noisy,
have to be somewhere affordable,
perhaps off that piazza in Trastevere
where we ate the grilled octopus—or *pol-*

po—I can still picture the waiter's face,
oh, what is the name of that place?

II

A *sonnet* contains exactly fourteen lines,
traditionally of iambic pentameter,
meaning "fifty feet of iambs" per line,
which is why so few can afford real meter

anymore. Then there is the "turn," or *volta,*
the hinge on which the poem's door
swings open, or shut, after the third stanza,
if Shakespearian, or the first if it's Petrossian, or—

anyway, those are the common variations.
It's either *sestet* and *octave,* eight plus six,
or a rhymed couplet preceded by three quatrains.
It all depends on which *stanza form* you pick.

Stanza, now *stanza,* in Italian, means, uhm—
hold on, we appear to have a problem. . . .

5. Broken Pantoum

In a pantoum lines flow like water down marble stairs.
But a pantoum is more like an escalator,
or a conveyor belt, than a staircase, if anyone cares.
A pantoum is more like an escalator

than an ocelot is like a butter bean, that's for sure!
Pantoum is the Malaysian word for "tedium."
Think Lawrence Welk and his waltzing cadavers.
Some forms are real hard, a pantoum is medium.

Pantoum is the Malaysian word for "tedium."
Like a conveyor belt, like a waltzing ocelot. Sure,
I like butter beans on toast, and eggs over medium.
Pantoum is Malaysian for "insomnia-cure."

Can you guess the Malay word for "mind-numbing"?
How about "plug my ears with butter beans"?
Could you even name the capital of Malaysia,
or find it on a map? Listen, I can tell

you'd like to waltz with me, and I'd like that a lot,
but it's obvious you're only pretending to care
that pantoum is the Malay word for "ocelot." Anyway,
I broke my damn pantoum falling down the stairs!

6. *Sestina to the Editors of* McSweeney's Internet Tendency, *and Vice Versa*

Your lamentable policy of publishing no poems but sestinas
insults your readers even as it patronizes contemporary American
    poetry.
To avoid depicting your magazine as a snake-nest of crypto-fascists
and avert the use of rash or unflattering language
on my part, I have reached the unusual and perhaps uncool
decision to donate to the editors of *McSweeney's Internet Tendency*

the remainder of this poem—to grant the editors of *McSweeney's Internet*
    Tendency
a platform from which to articulate their defense. "Yo, what's wrong
    with sestinas!
We think sestinas are totally, totally cool!
In Brooklyn and SF sestinas are easily the coolest form of poetry
out there today. Especially we love the way the language
cascades obsessively from stanza to stanza, a kind of crypto-Ashberian

waterfall of language, actually, or hey, crypto-formalists
can wing it too, we can handle that, the editors of *McSweeney's Internet*
    Tendency
dig that Elizabeth Bishop thing. L=A=N=G=U=A=G=E
Poetry, now that's another kettle of polliwogs—not that sestinas
could ever be considered as Language Poetry,
could they? Or, would that maybe be wildly inventive and cool?

Cool cool cool cool cool cool cool cool cool cool.

It might look like that on the page, kind of crypto-Dadaist,

but should it be punctuated? Is there some kind of Language Poetry

Manual of Style the editors of *McSweeney's Internet Tendency*

might employ to ensure these killer new language poetry sestinas

are abiding by the rules? Whatever. I mean, language

is not bound by laws, right, there is no binding legal language

language itself cannot delegitimize? Which is, like, beyond cool.

What really matters here is form, that funky, prismatic, six-fold way

    sestinas

have of origamying into shape on the page, their crypto-Buddhist

vibe. We flat-out love that. The editors of *McSweeney's Internet Tendency*

have created a very hip magazine, even if it is virtual, and poetry

is part of that, and frankly you should be thankful we publish *any*

    poetry

because, mostly, the stuff sucks. Dude, what's it all about—language?

Hello, what isn't? The editors of *McSweeney's Internet Tendency*

know what's cool—we are, basically, the arbiters of cool—

and we really don't need a bunch of wonkified, cry-baby crypto-elitists

preaching to us about the perceived demerits or what-all of sestinas."

The Editors of McSweeney's Internet Tendency *regret that your poetry*

is not cool enough for them at this time. They felt the language

fell flat, unfortunately. Next time try a crypto-sestina.

NOTES ON LANGUAGE AND MEANING

To drape the damp beach towel of language
upon the aluminum lawn chair of meaning
is neither more nor less admirable
than laying it across the chaise lounge of non-meaning,
to say nothing of abandoning it in a sodden heap
soaked with pool water and orange Fanta.

•

Once the egg of meaning has been smashed
the mystery lies revealed: to smear
the walls with yolk is extraneous, and impolite.

•

Too often the wit of disjuncture
resembles a puzzle made of lettuce.

•

Driving to work I cross six bridges and a causeway
to the mainland: still, when the drawbridge opens,
I am surprised again at the sight of water.

•

You cannot teach a person to be a whale,
but you can bring them to see the beauty of whales;
you can present whales to their attention,
whales in their actual selves, and so the lesson is learned.

And those who do not perceive the beauty,
those who would kill and boil and render them?

You cannot teach a person to be a whale.

•

To decry the flawed mechanics of language
is not to assert the desirability
of abandoning mechanical engineering altogether:

highways made from taffy and flower stems
are unlikely to sustain the traffic of substantiation,
let alone the Memphis blues again.

•

Do not blame Wittgenstein for problems
foisted upon us by Derrida and Bob Dylan.

•

If the constellations were drawn by hand
they might resemble sleeping cheetahs:
still we find the faces of those we love
have grown older in the morning.

ESSAY ON NOVELS

Their shambling power and verisimilitude,
their mimetic resemblance to souvenir Yuletide
snowstorm paperweights in which we discover
our elfin selves shoveling silver glitter,

or scrimshawed whale's teeth, or
ships-in-bottles, or breath-fogged mirrors,

fanciful, delimited, craft-wise, time-bound,
toothsome and foredoomed as mastodons
crossing the tundra page by page
through the last ecstatic blizzard of the Ice Age.

POETRY AND FICTION

Their affair has been tempestuous,
and then some. Like us

they like to get it on,
to rut and hump, bang a gong,

but then grow sullen,
wondering not if but when

the end will come. He says to her:
You're not all pretty flowers

and hippie skirts, bitch!
And she: *If you want to switch*

genres go buy a thesaurus,
don't just mope around all morose

and quasi-narrative. And so it goes.
They criticize each other's clothes,

her eye for art, his ear for music,
then they hit the sack,

and pledge to give it one more chance.
Theirs is a heterotextual romance.

TIGER HUNTING WITH ROBERT LOWELL

We were several hours into our journey, traveling through a mixture of teak forest and open savannah, mounted on the Maharajah's royal elephant with its fabulously jeweled livery, and I must have dozed off for a while, because Lowell was suddenly holding forth on poetry, which had not, so far as I was aware, been the subject of our previous conversation. "Poets are like Marxists, consuming themselves in splinter-groups and petty factions, a nest of snakes contesting the minutiae of tactics and rhetoric while the world carries on in blissful ignorance of their monumental struggles and long-awaited triumphs. Much like the princes and rajas when the British arrived in India," he continued professorially, "worried only about seizing advantage from their rivals, until before long every one of them was under the thumb of a fat woman named Victoria back in London." Lowell wiped his forehead and took a swig from an emerald-crusted flask I had first noticed at the Maharajah's palace. "And now," he continued, beginning to emit a strange, strangled wail, "I will summon our prey using the secret call of the Bengal tiger—*weelawaugh, we-ee-eelawaugh, weelawaugh!*"

"How is it you learned to hunt tigers, Cal," I inquired, "in New England?"

"Same way I learned to harpoon a whale," Lowell replied. "From Uncle Winslow, more or less. But wait!" He held up his hand for quiet, listening intently, and as he did I became aware of a clamorous hubbub coming along the trail behind us, and looking back observed a party of the Maharajah's men making haste along it, greatly agitated, indeed, shouting and gesticulating in our direction. "The tiger will come this way," Lowell said, seemingly unaware of our pursuers, motioning generally at the expanse of shoulder-high grass we had paused amidst. "Be ready." My chances of shooting a tiger were nil, but luckily Lowell, who described himself as a crack shot, exhibited complete confidence in his abilities. "A natural sharpshooter," he explained. "A child prodigy. Like something out of Fenimore Cooper."

"Are those the trackers?" I asked, pointing to the excited throng now actually running towards us in their variously colored turbans and uniforms. "Because they're in the wrong place."

Taking notice, at last, of the approaching mob, Lowell appeared momentarily startled, then hitched his leg over the riding platform, clambered onto the elephant's back and slid down its massive flank to the ground, where he began to disrobe. "We did have permission," I began, a bit hesitant to bring up the unpleasantness back at the palace, "we did have permission to take the royal elephant, didn't we, Cal?" "More or less," he replied, rubbing mud across his neck and chest. He dropped his trousers and slapped clay-colored swaths of dirt across his pale calves and thighs. "At this time the hunt shall continue on foot. Precisely as Uncle Winslow would have wished!" Lowell saluted me crisply, then bowed formally from the waist. "Call me Ishmael," he whispered, disappearing into the long grass just as the Maharajah's men arrived in the clearing, swatting at my legs with their sticks, and pulled me from my perch on the back of that splendid beast, and the serious beatings began.

ELIZABETH BISHOP:
DEPARTURE FROM SANTOS

Awful to blame the climate for all this
blissful misery, to call the fetid, fretful tropics
Cupid and pin the rap on scissor-tailed frigate birds
dicing equatorial sunsets into unescorted paper dolls.

Enter, stage left, the fateful cashew,
fruit of Eros' insubordinate womb: wave a warm
goodbye to all those frigid Nova Scotian taboos,
hauled off on Labrador's icy current to Greenland's fjords or
Iceland's odor of herring and sulphur,
jury-rigged dories bound for sub-Arctic islets.

Kah-zhu. Like a sneeze in Chinese,
like a summer home for Kubla Khan as Coleridge
might have had it, had not he lost it,
narcotically enrapt, at a knock upon the door.

O, where is my very own
Person of Porlock to stem this lugubrious tide!

Quayside, no doubt, booking her passage,
readying to reboard that trusty steed,
S.S. *Abandonment.*

Thus ends my sojourn on Crusoe's cloud-dump.
Uneternally yours, my dearliest Friday,
very warmest regards, et cetera. It appears
we are under way already, or it is under us.
Xanadu is no place for such ladies or downfallen
Yankees as we, eh, Miss Breen? And she:
Zanzibar? Now there is an enchanting island!

PO BIZ

It is all too true that jolly old A is a careerist hack
who couldn't write his way out of a paper bag,
and that B's emotional interior is a landscape
modeled upon William Blake's etchings of Hell.

C is generally considered a gnomish charlatan,
while D is a charming woman whose work
nonetheless resembles a turkey carcass
picked at by raccoons the day after Thanksgiving.

E and F have come to detest each other so deeply
that the program they co-direct is a viper pit
of venomous epithets and flying paperweights,
while poor G spouts self-realization aphorisms

like some kind of Yeatsian scripture.
H is a backstabbing, megalomaniacal quisling.
I is a poseur. And J is openly derided as a stick-bug
tethered to the titanic parade float of his ego.

None of which merits the least consideration here
because it is the work alone that matters,
the coarse, oaten bread and nectar-swizzled fruit of poetry
that will sustain us long after the grant committee

has emailed its rejection (by the way, check out
who's on that committee, yet again, no surprise).
So I will not pour forth the cheap wine of innuendo,
I will not dot the rumor-monger's *i*'s

or cross the idle gossip's *t*'s
by discussing what happened that infamous night
on the balcony at the AWP convention.
I will not recycle the tales of W's institutionalization

or X's adulterous escapades in Prague
(. . . and, ahem, Iowa City).
Why Y got fired is nobody's business
and how she got rehired remains a head-scratcher,

but don't eat spaghetti with your hands at Bread Loaf,
and never ask students to disrobe *even partially*
are rules we can all live by,
and will long remember, thanks to Z.

NOTES ON PROCESS

Revision

What does it say about my critical vision
that whenever I get a bad haircut,
which is not infrequently,
I spend the next three days searching out
hanks of hair that feel wrong,
consulting the mirror, and clipping away?
Invariably these corrections serve only
to make a difficult situation worse.
In which I resemble William Wordsworth.

Metaphor

To brandish a transfigurative flame,
to rise out of the self costumed in symbols,
like the businessman coming late to his meeting
caught in the beam of the PowerPoint projector.

Ambition

Like the squirrel leaping wildly from tree to tree amid the luxuriant foliage of May—is he escaping a predator, chasing a mate, or simply enjoying himself, shaking in turn all the limbs of the sycamore, catalpa, maple and elm?

Language

Uh.

Transitions

As when the hero comes over the hill and sees the road ahead barricaded by police vehicles, and pauses, asking himself, implicitly, well, should I hit the gas and go for it, ending this journey in a hail of bullets and exploding gas tanks—or perhaps, miraculously, forcing a passage, swerving through, free and clear, to disappear around the bend, en route to the next unforeseen, picaresque adventure? Or should I come forward slowly, try to talk my way through? What is my infraction, after all—what actions have I undertaken that any self-respecting poem would not have taken in my place? Yes, that's the thing to do, surrender peacefully, trust to the authorities, it will all work out in the end. Like that moment. And then the smell of burning rubber as he jams the pedal to the floor.

Ego

> Sinew scraped from the flesh
> and strung, essence
> of the self gibbeted and hung
>
> self/meme melody/theme

Images

as the mind follows an idea into the music
and builds its temple there

as a sculptor stirs her coffee with a tin spoon filmed in marble dust

as across the globe of a lover's breast
a finger circles
the realization of its destiny

Publication

Like the morning after the birthday party
when Mylar balloons
tug against their token earth-weights
inflecting the streamers of silver sunlight
with the sadness
and urgency of their desire
to rise.

SANDBURG VARIATIONS

i. *Early Spring*

Money courses through Chicago's veins like the essence urging the red-buds into bloom, tulips made wiser by the memory of snow, template of April and the daffodils paper-hung, bereft, the white whale of winter rendered unto fat. And May, the grape hyacinth, apple blossom—and the rain ruining the west-facing azaleas while the north-facing azaleas have yet to bloom. You can feel it pulsing along the industrious avenues, viscid, luxuriant, explosively amoral—the old neighborhood flush with it now, the industrial bakery torn down, sad tracts of mud and cinders, cairns of crumbled brick behind barbed-wire. Like an animal breathing, veins of a leaf running with sap, engine of effulgence, resurgent, branches and limbs and roots and blossoms, a force beyond reason, or ruthlessly reasonable.

ii. *Prairie School*

Chicago's magnificent cubic scatter across the snow-sketched prairie,
its arrowing ascension and continental horizontality,
its railyard conjury and truckway bricolage,
its voluble thrum of human self-assurance—

discourse of happenstance or absolute mastery,
monologue of the jackal as known on Kedzie, Pulaski, Cicero,
street rant of the prophet roaming those wide, western avenues
cloaked in an aurora of enlightenment or psychosis.

iii. Aubade

Which among us has never heard the music of traffic taking wing, shades and variations of a logarithmic chord, song of the city like a message from within? Who could fail the summons of yon quite visible smokestacks aglint through grey inutterable vapors this peculiarly unparticular morn? Where is he who does not bear the scars of shingle nails upon a tattered thumb, the tar of Stinky Weinberg's stooped roof, laundromats raped and looted by streetlights, busses smoked to fitful ashes, night's metropolis melted down and recast? Song of the city like a terrible job, nail-gunning sheetrock in a West Loop heat wave, late shift with a push broom in a clockless terminal, hustling cocktails at zero hour when the sour beads of fear drop like pearl onions into every glass of beer and watered whiskey along the rail, sad drunks eating pickled eggs, loneliness worn like the robes of a prize fighter, rags and bones, rags and what?

iv. For Those Begging Spare Change Outside the Chicago Board of Trade

The ghosts of Chicago are not immaterial, they are not sad or lost.
They wander among us, worldly and explicit.
They fear the hawk and speak respectfully of the mayor.

Hoping for nickels their laces flap open, pockets full
of pint bottles and luckless Lotto tickets.

Numbers do not tell their story, nor the rattle
of disconsolate coins in paper cups,
nor the wall behind them with its monument to men at work
in a more just republic and a century of simpler labor.

Their song is not the wind but an insistent click of longing
I've heard all day, every block of the city, every footfall,
until, on a bench near the lake at evening,
I discover embedded in the heel of my boot
a battered lapel pin in the shape of the American flag.

Sitting alone in a bar in West Virginia watching *Monday Night Football*, I come to consider the beauty of bartenders and their metaphorical resemblance to angels. Today's incarnation is Fallon, streak of white dyed in her jet-black hair, now doing shots at the bar with Rick, her sometimes boyfriend, who loves above all else playing music, always at it, only missed three days of practice in the last two years and that to go fishing with his brother. Rick is learning funk bass to accompany the bluegrass guitar he cut his teeth on back home in Nashville, which explains why he keeps requesting songs by the Red Hot Chili Peppers. *Lord, nobody in the entire state of Tennessee but plays in a band, singing about lions and buried treasure and the sweet flesh of the beloved.* Rick tells me he was born in 1984 and I tell him that in 1985 I saw the Red Hot Chili Peppers play these very songs at a club in New York City, a fact alluded to in a poem I read earlier this evening to a roomful of college students, many of whom, never having been to a poetry reading before, asked me as they exited to sign my name on their Xeroxed programs, either to prove their attendance for extra credit or as if it were the autograph of a minor celebrity, a versifying Red Hot Chili Pepper descended from the library shelf. We are not far from James Wright's hometown, which can no longer afford to celebrate its famous son with the touchingly sentimental Poetry Festival named in his honor, a literary event unlike any other in this country, held in the very library in which he discovered the books that enabled his escape from that town of retired factory hands on front porch lawn chairs, a town of abandoned mills and bars not unlike this one wedged between the railroad tracks and the Ohio River. A good-looking bartender is a dangerous benefactor, bestower of mercy and of temptation in like measure. Mercy which may also be oblivion. Next week I'll be sitting in a bar in Central Europe drinking the local pilsner named after a golden pheasant, which I believe without ever having tasted to be delicious. Faith in the instruments and their servants, faith in good beer to come, faith that the Cowboys will lose, as they do, on a field goal in overtime. Draw a circle—whatever's inside it is the poem. Everything else is the world. Keep drawing that circle larger and larger, keep going, keep going. This poem was written on the back of a Jack Daniel's coaster at a bar in Morgantown, West Virginia, which may, after all, explain a few things.

POEM THAT NEEDS NO INTRODUCTION

i.

Listen, I have endured so much bad art in my lifetime
that my brain actually throbs and pulses
in the manner of a 1960s comic book supervillain
and my skull threatens to burst at the seams like a lychee nut
at the mere thought of all those tuneless bands and lousy etchings
and earnest readings in coffeehouses
smelling of clove cigarettes,
pretentious photos of phallomorphic icebergs,
the opening at the gallery hung with stillborn elephants—
what could you say?—and one unforgettable night
a conceptual dance performance akin to a ritual sacrifice
with the audience as victims—as if art
might prove the literal death of me—all this,
all this and so much more,
only to find myself here, in Bratislava,
at the Ars Poetica poetry festival,
yet again drinking red wine from a plastic cup
while the poets declaim in languages
dense and indecipherable as knotted silk, thinking, well,
what could be better than this?

ii.

Perhaps it would be better if the air conditioning worked
and the keg of *Zlaty Bazant* had not run dry

but the local wine is unexpectedly delicious, hearty as wild boar's blood,
and the very existence of such an exuberantly cacophonous conclave
in this diminutive and innocuous backwater of *Mittel Europa*
makes me yearn to do something hearty and wine-soaked and boarish—
no, not boorish—to shout spontaneous bebop musings
like the hipster Beatnik poet Fred from Paris
or crack wise like the balding Frank O'Hara imitator from Vienna
or sing like the yodeling, pop-eyed jokester from Prague
or simply intone with great seriousness like the well-mannered poets
from Warsaw and Wroclaw, Berlin and Budapest and Brno.

iii.

o river sand,
sink deeper and fling yourself
into my whirlpool!

blue sunflower gas-ring octopus—
what brings you
to the rain forest, amigo?

iv.

Well, that came out a bit like Basho imitating Corso
but the thought is what counts when it is 10:45 and you are drunk
enough to believe a poem scribbled on a festival program
could change the world

and when someone says time is an invisible marauder

I shout *Fuck you!* and everybody smiles.

v.

This poem will change the world.

This poem is a revolutionary anthem to global insurrection.

This poem is an international pop sensation, over twenty million sold.

This poem saved the baby from the burning building.

This poem knows how to howl, to hoot like an owl.

This poem refuses to throw in the towel.

This poem is an imposter, down with this poem!

This poem has been weaponized.

I am breathing its evil fumes, its paralytic murk.

This poem twists my arm until I cry uncle.

This poem will never help me no matter how much I beg.

Help me, please, somebody help me!

This poem wants to kick some ass.

This poem is going to mess you up so bad.

This poem will bury you, my friend.

vi.

But this poem really digs your sister, with her pigtails
and her songs about polar bears and fast rides to immortality,
your sister is someone to run away with to live
in a castle in a dark Teutonic forest or a cheap apartment
with no furniture but a futon and typewriter in the city
underneath the city that is underneath this city.

vii.

Take a swig of wine and it is 12:15.
Another and it is ten past two.

Fuck you!

But where was I?
Ah yes, Bratislava.

viii.

At the Mayor's Palace we are instructed to visit the Apple Festival,
a "new tradition" created by the Ministry of Culture
modeled upon the actual traditions of the Slovak country folk
who feel, one can only assume, quite strongly about their apples.

Try as we might we cannot find any sign of the festival

and when we return to the Ministry of Culture

the woman at the desk denies any knowledge of it.

Not to worry, she says, next week begins the Cabbage Festival.

ix.

And tonight is the big national soccer match

and the exuberant crowd watching on jumbo screens in the square

is drinking Coca-Cola from minuscule aluminum cans provided by
    girls

in red jumpsuits and Afro wigs as a promotion but where was I?

Ah yes, art—art is what we came for and what we got

was a reminder that this is how it begins, no, not in fright wigs

but a communion of scars and charms and midnight plunder,

a reminder that even our most profound individual suffering

amounts to little more than ashes on the grate of a city

engulfed in eternal flames, which is certainly not this charming

metropolis of beer gardens and trolleys and long-haired Slavic angels

whose golden swords glitter madly above the Danube at dawn.

x.

Ladies and gentlemen, the bar is now closed.

You've been a wonderful audience
and I want to thank you all
for coming tonight
and to leave you with one last piece,
if I can find the right page, ah yes, here we go.

This is a poem that needs no introduction.

THE BURNING SHIP

No room for regret or self-doubt in art,
doubt but not self-doubt. The ship hauls anchor,
the kerosene lantern flickers and goes out,
voices in the pitch black swell with anger

as shipmates mistake each other for enemies.
The lantern spills, the pilot drops a lit cigar.
Tragedy ensues and engenders more tragedy.
If only the moon could see, if only the stars

had been granted the power of speech.
But the blind remain blind, the voiceless mute.
The burning ship threads its way between reefs
in the darkness. Doubt, but not self-doubt.

THE CATTLE RAID

Poetry is not an island unto itself.

It is a free republic, a proud and independent realm, but it does not stand alone. We citizens must share this fertile land with our neighbors—a few, several, many; their number varies, their configurations shift with the passing years as ancient fiefdoms grow impoverished and young city-states amass great wealth, new nations are born and principalities disintegrate into warring factions—though these are merely political distinctions, as is widely understood, and the ground beneath our feet is continuous, extending in every direction to the horizon. It is a beautiful island and we ought upon awakening sing its praises to the rising sun, as it is said the cattle did, in times gone by, the cattle of the Republic of Poetry being anciently gifted with the power of human speech.

Life on the island is straightforward: I do not say easy, but simple enough.

Of the several nations, poetry is the most time-honored, its roots descending beyond historical record. It possesses many fine monuments and ruins of past glory. It is largely peaceable. It harbors no malice towards its neighbors. It supports no standing army nor does it seek to copyright its wisdom. Golden birds sing in its branches, golden minarets glint on distant hills, yet from the legendary power of antiquity it is much reduced.

The problem is not one of essential properties, but of power politics;

not of grazing lands, but of cows.

Our herds are diminished, for we are surrounded by neighbors who profess their esteem even as they steal our cattle!

The Republic of Poetry has been generous to a fault; too courteous, too reliant on diplomacy, too focused on internal squabbles, we have grown lax in our vigilance.

It is in light of this sad reduction of our estate that the following proposal is put forth:

That we, in our turn, sally forth to steal the cattle of our neighbors.

That we shift our attention outward, find what is valuable around us, and carry it back across the border—not merely for personal gain but to enrich the coffers of the realm.

A good day raiding the borderlands of the Kingdom of Fiction could reclaim stray calves even as we re-annex our long-contested grazing lands; by moonlight we might pilfer from the Realm of Biography, while from the vast Empire of History we could hope to wrest entire territories in time. A well-aimed lasso in Natural Sciences yields a stray longhorn, while a foray into the Peoples' Republic of the Social Sciences supplies the breeding stock for an anthropological poetry of civilization, a psychological poetry of self-realization, a sociological poetry of the self in context. Returning by way of the Highlands of the

Primary Texts, we can range the moors in search of the wild aurochs of Etymology, seek out the beasts of pure form in the dales and hollows of Myth.

Crowded grow the stockyards of Romance, Mystery, SciFi and Self-Help!

How many fine milk cows graze within the fenced fields of Folk Tales, Essays, Memoir!

We might leave a thousand for every one we take and still our herds would swell!

Be fearless, fellow riders!

Cross all borders!

If those from whom you steal choose to quarrel, remember that they were all our cattle once, and none should begrudge a past benefactor simple sustenance. Even among our own folk some will resist what you bring, having grown inward-looking, forgetful of the extension of our former glory, while others will never return from the raid at all, choosing to settle on the wide plains of the Novel, in the salubrious vineyards of the Short Story—

but you shall have nothing to fear.

Even if the posse tracks you down, how can they stop a message of such purity?

Because it need not be written, it cannot be censored; because it need not be spoken, it cannot be silenced. There is no poetry jail—and if there were, you could compose your poems secure in its solitude—and they cannot exile you from the Island of Language because, by definition, its limits comprise the limits of our world.

Here we must confront the issue of boundaries and surveys, the mystery of Terra Incognita.

No authoritative exploration of this place has been undertaken; we imagine it as an island, but there is no map or chart to delimit it, though it is not limitless. Travel far enough in any direction and you will come to a shoreline, in sight of which lie tumbled rocks and foundering shoals, raw islets that serve as rookeries for seabirds, and against the grey horizon an unknown number of other lands, places terrible or marvelous toward which, with good weather and stout craft, a voyage of discovery might be launched.

What songs, what tales, what adventures await the brave of heart who undertake such journeys.

What cattle we might find—indigo zebu, velvet-skinned Brahmans with horns of titanium alloy.

It is true, they come from across the water, and we have as yet found no means of translating their silence into poetry. But a herdsman's life demands patience, vision and patience. For now we shall set them to graze on the fine grass of our renowned pasturelands, let them wander the hills and river bottoms, mingling with the local herd, learning their ways.

One fine morning they will come to us, at daybreak, singing.